W9-AVJ-727

HYDRA

DO YOU BELIEVE?

This series features creatures that excite our minds. They're magical. They're mythical. They're mysterious. They're also not real. They live in our stories. They're brought to life by our imaginations. Facts about these creatures are based on folklore, legends, and beliefs. We have a rich history of believing in the impossible. But these creatures only live in fantasies and dreams. Monsters do not live under our beds. They live in our heads!

45th Parallel Press

Published in the United States of America by Cherry Lake Publishing
Ann Arbor, Michigan
www.cherrylakepublishing.com

Reading Adviser: Marla Conn MS, Ed., Literacy specialist, Read-Ability, Inc.
Book Design: Felicia Macheske

Photo Credits: © Kostyantyn Ivanyshen/Shutterstock.com, cover; © Sofia Santos/Shutterstock.com, 1;
© Oksana Golubeva/Shutterstock.com, 5; © Atelier Sommerland/Shutterstock.com, 7; © YUSRAN ABDUL
RAHMAN/Shutterstock.com, 9; © Heritage Images/ Getty Images, 10; © andreiuc88/Shutterstock.com, 13;
© Daniel Caluian/Shutterstock.com, 15; © NikoNomad/iStock, 16; © Vuk Kostic/Shutterstock.com, 19;
© isoga/Shutterstock.com, 20; © Nejron Photo/Shutterstock.com, 22; © Lena_graphics/iStock, 25; © Mauro
Carli/Shutterstock.com, 27; © Dan Exton/Shutterstock.com, 28

Graphic Elements Throughout: © denniro/Shutterstock.com; © Libellule/Shutterstock.com; © sociologas/
Shutterstock.com; © paprika/Shutterstock.com; © ilolab/Shutterstock.com; © Bruce Rolff/Shutterstock.com

45th Parallel Press is an imprint of Cherry Lake Publishing.

Library of Congress Cataloging-in-Publication Data

Names: Loh-Hagan, Virginia, author.
Title: Hydra / by Virginia Loh-Hagan.
Description: Ann Arbor : Cherry Lake Publishing, 2016. | Series: Magic, myth,
 and mystery | Includes bibliographical references and index.
Identifiers: LCCN 2016005103| ISBN 9781634711142 (hardcover) | ISBN
 9781634712132 (pdf) | ISBN 9781634713122 (pbk.) | ISBN 9781634714112 (ebook)
Subjects: LCSH: Hydra (Greek mythology)–Juvenile literature.
Classification: LCC BL820.H93 L64 2016 | DDC 398.20938/0454–dc23
LC record available at http://lccn.loc.gov/2016005103

Cherry Lake Publishing would like to acknowledge the work of The Partnership for 21st Century Skills.
Please visit *www.p21.org* for more information.

Printed in the United States of America
Corporate Graphics Inc.

TABLE of CONTENTS

Many Monster Heads

Who was Hydra? What other monster is like Hydra?

"Two heads are better than one." This is an old saying. Hydra was a sea monster. Most say she had nine heads. But some believe she had thousands of heads.

Hydra lived in Lake Lerna. It was in ancient Greece. It was like a swamp. She lived in an underwater cave. It was a gate to the **underworld**. The underworld is where people went after they died. Hydra was its guard.

She stayed close to the lake. But she had to eat. She'd leave the lake. She went into town. She hunted. She killed. She ate animals. She ate people.

Hydra's lair was the entrance to the underworld.

Explained by Science!

Hydra had extreme bad breath. Humans get it as well. The condition is called halitosis. Twenty percent of humans have it. Halitosis doesn't kill people. But it keeps people away. It could mean tooth decay. It could mean sickness. The smell is caused by bacteria. Bacteria sits below the gum line. It's also on the back of the tongue. People with halitosis might have a "white tongue." They need to take care of their mouths. They need to brush their teeth. They need to scrape their tongues. They need to use dental floss. They need to use mouthwash. They may need medicine.

Medusa is a monster similar to Hydra.

Hydra was like a **dragon**. It's a mythical monster. It's like a giant reptile. Hydra had a snake's body. She had two arms. She had two legs.

Hydra is sometimes mistaken for Scylla. Scylla was pretty. She was a water spirit. The sea god liked her. His wife got jealous. She poisoned Scylla's bathwater. Scylla became a water monster. She had 12 legs. She had a cat's tail. She had six long necks. She had six dog heads. Each mouth had three rows of sharp teeth. She attacked ships.

Chapter Two

Kill or be Killed

What did Hydra look like?
What were Hydra's powers?

Hydra is scarier than Scylla. Hydra lived to kill. Her job was to guard Lerna. She was a trained killer.

She had many heads. She was hard to kill. She had super healing powers. She could **regenerate**. This means she could regrow body parts. If she lost a head, she'd grow more heads. She grew two heads for every one lost head. This happened quickly. She could keep attacking. She never got tired.

Hydra's heads are like an octopus or squid's tentacles.

Each head had many sharp teeth. She'd bite. She'd tear. She'd rip. Each head had sharp horns. She'd ram. She'd punch. Some heads made fire. Some heads spit magical water. She could blast her enemies. She'd send them flying.

She had one main head. It was in the middle. This head was **immortal**. This meant it could never die. It could live forever. It lived after being cut off. It couldn't be harmed.

She used her long necks. She'd lunge. She could attack from different positions.

Some stories give Hydra more tails, arms, or wings.

When Fantasy Meets Reality!

A hydra is a real animal. It lives in fresh water. It lives in the tropics. It's small. It's less than 0.5 inches (1.3 centimeters) long. It's shaped like a tube. It moves like an inchworm. It doesn't have a brain or muscles. It's a bundle of nerves. It's related to jellyfish. It has about 12 thin tentacles coming out of its mouth. Tentacles are like arms. They have stingers. The stingers paralyze prey. A hydra can regenerate. It can regrow body parts. It doesn't appear to age. It doesn't appear to die of old age. It seems to live forever.

A sleeping Hydra could kill passersby with her snores.

Hydra had poison. Her poison caused much pain before death. Her blood was poisonous. She used her fangs. She injected poison. Her breath was stinky. It was poisonous. Just smelling it was deadly. The path of her breath was deadly. Her spit was poisonous. She spit **acid**. Acid is dangerous. It burns through things. It destroys things.

She had sharp claws. She had sharp spikes on her spines. She had a long tail. She was a strong fighter. Her body had lots of weapons.

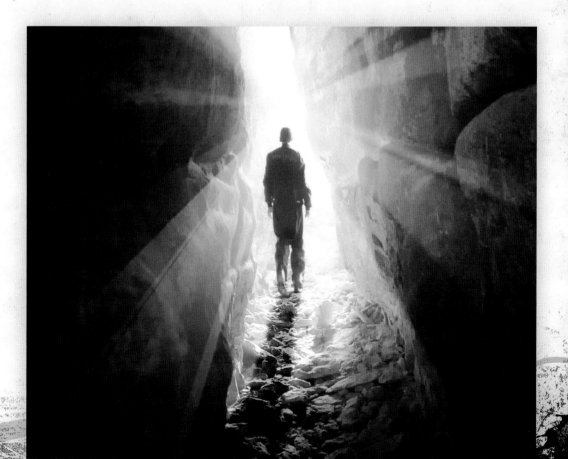

Chapter Three

Death by Hercules

Who was Hercules? What were Hydra's weaknesses?

Hercules was half-man. He was half-god. He was the strongest human. He **slayed** Hydra. Slay means to kill. He had to complete 12 tasks. Slaying Hydra was his second task.

He went to Lerna. He used a cloth. He covered his mouth. He covered his nose. He used a sword. He cut Hydra's heads. But her heads kept growing back. He asked for help. His nephew was with him. Hercules chopped off heads. His nephew burned the neck stumps. This stopped new heads from growing.

Hercules also tried using a club to slay Hydra.

Hydra's many heads confused people.

Hydra became weak. She needed all her heads. Her heads hid her main head.

Hercules saw Hydra's immortal head. He chopped it off. It was still alive. He buried it. He placed a big rock over it.

Hercules dipped his arrows in Hydra's blood. Later, he used the arrows to kill a **centaur**. A centaur is a human with a horse body. Later, Hercules touched the poisoned blood. He died. So, Hydra actually killed Hercules, too.

SURVIVAL TIPS!

- Wear a head mask. Cover the eyes. Cover the mouth. Cover the nose. Avoid Hydra's breath.

- Get a scythe. It has a long curved blade.

- Don't try to tame Hydra. She can't be controlled. It'd be like training a pack of wolves.

- Trap her. Use yourself as bait. Lead her into a cage. Then, run away. Let other people kill her.

- Fight Hydra on land. Don't let her go into water. She's a strong swimmer. Plus, she can breathe underwater. (You can't.)

- Attack as a team. Work together. Hydra is hard to kill alone.

Chapter Four

All in the Family

Who were Hydra's parents? Who were her siblings?

Echidna was Hydra's mother. She was the "mother of monsters." She was half-woman. She was half-snake. She lived in a cave. She lived alone. She had snakes for hair. She ate raw flesh.

Typhon was Hydra's father. He was the "father of monsters." He was a giant. His legs were snake coils. He hissed as he moved. He had glowing red eyes. He had 100 dragon heads. The heads spit fire. They

made a lot of noise. He had hundreds of wings.
His fingers were dead snakes.

Hydra got her looks from her parents.

Typhon didn't fit in with the other gods. He didn't like that. He wanted to take over. He fought the king of the gods. He lost. He was punished. He was jailed under a mountain.

He married Echidna. They had many monster children. They wanted their children to cause humans harm. This means Hydra had **siblings**. Siblings are sisters and brothers.

The Nemean Lion was Hydra's brother. He had sharp claws. He had magical fur. Weapons couldn't kill him. But Hercules tricked him. He strangled him. He killed him. He used the Nemean Lion's claw to skin him.

Typhon tries to get free. That's why we have earthquakes.

Chimera was Hydra's sister. She breathed fire. She was a lion. She had a goat head coming out of her back. Her tail was a snake.

Cerberus was Hydra's brother. Like Hydra, he guarded the underworld. He didn't let people escape. He was a dog. He had three heads. His tail was a snake. Snake heads came out of his back.

Hydra didn't grow up with her family. The queen of the gods took Hydra. She wanted Hydra to guard Lerna. She raised Hydra to fight Hercules.

Lions, snakes, and dragons are closely related in the monster world.

Know the Lingo!

- **Appendages:** limbs

- **Cetus:** sea monster similar to a whale

- **Fate:** predestined turn of events

- **Fury:** uncontrollable anger

- **Gorgon:** ugly female monster whose gaze turned men to stone

- **Hades:** ruler of the underworld

- **Harpy:** female monster with a bird body and human face

- **Hippocamp:** mythical sea horse

- **Kraken:** giant squid monster

- **Naiads:** water nymphs

- **Nemesis:** enemy

- **Poseidon:** ruler of the seas

- **Sea hag:** sea witch

- **Serpent:** snake

- **Sirens:** pretty female monsters that cause shipwrecks by singing

- **Zeus:** ruler of the sky, king of the gods

Chapter Five

More Hydra Monsters

What are other versions of Hydra?

Many cultures have stories about Hydra. The Greeks have the most popular version.

Japan's Hydra was called Orochi. She had eight heads. She had eight tails. She had red eyes. She had trees growing on her back. She was a giant snake. Susanoo was a storm god. He met a couple. The couple was crying. Orochi had demanded their daughters. Susanoo helped them. He tricked Orochi. He cut Orochi into pieces. The couple's daughters were saved.

Greek myths are stories that explain something.

Real-World Connection

Some humans have more than one head. This condition is called polycephaly. Abby and Brittany Hensel are conjoined twins. They share one body. They have a wide chest. They're joined. But they have separate heads. They have separate hearts. They have separate stomachs. They have separate lungs. They have separate spines. Each girl controls one arm. Each girl controls one leg. They work together to walk, clap, type, and drive. Abby said, "We take turns." They were born in Minnesota. Their mom is a nurse. Their dad is a carpenter. The parents chose not to separate them at birth. One twin would've died. The twins said, "We were raised to believe we could do anything we wanted to do."

Christians have a Hydra story. Hydra was a dragon. She had two legs. She had seven heads. Each head represented a deadly sin. (There are seven deadly sins.) Saint Michael slayed her.

Saint Michael was an angel. He was the leader of God's army. He fought against evil. He fought a war in heaven. He led angels into battle. He fought against the dragon. He put his spear into the dragon's heads. He won. He kicked the dragon out of heaven.

Hydra represented evil. She was from the dark side.

There's a Hydra story in Africa. Hydra was a male monster. He had seven heads. He kept the river flowing.

A woman asked Hydra for help. Hydra helped. But he wanted her daughter. The daughter's name was Jinde. Jinde went to the river. Hydra grabbed her. He married her. Jinde begged to see her family. Hydra let her go for one day. Jinde asked her boyfriend for help. Her boyfriend used his sword. He cut off Hydra's heads. Hydra died.

Hydra may get slain. But Hydra legends live on.

Hydra monsters lived in water.

Did You Know?

- Hera was a Greek goddess. She was the queen of the gods. She turned Hydra into a constellation. Hydra is the largest constellation. It's also the longest. It looks like a water snake. It's located in the area of the sky known as "the sea."

- Hydra is used as a real word. It means a hard problem. Hydras are hard to solve. When one problem is solved, other problems occur.

- Hydra is often called the Lernean Hydra.

- Hercules slayed the Nemean Lion before Hydra. He used its skin as protection.

- In some stories, Hydra's last head turned into a jewel.

- Hercules's teacher gave him advice. He recalled the advice before slaying Hydra. The advice was, "We rise by kneeling. We conquer by surrendering. We gain by giving up." This is why he asked for help.

- Albertus Seba collected animals. He called it his "cabinet of curiosities." He wrote a book. He included a picture of "The Hamburg Hydra." Carl Linnaeus proved it was fake. The Hydra was made from weasel heads and snake skins.

- Hydra had many heads. Ancient Greek painters couldn't paint all her heads on a vase.

- Hydra is the name of an island. It's in Greece. No wheeled vehicles are allowed. People ride donkeys.

Consider This!

Take a Position: Some people think Hydra is based on octopuses. Octopuses can regrow lost limbs. Octopus tentacles could be mistaken for Hydra's heads. People didn't know what octopuses were. So they created Hydra stories. What do you think about the connections between Hydra and octopuses? Do you think Hydra is really an octopus? Argue your point with reasons and evidence.

Say What? Many believe Hydra is a dragon. She's mistaken for other dragons. Read the 45th Parallel Press book about dragons. Explain how Hydra is similar to dragons. Explain how Hydra is different from dragons.

Think About It! Most stories define Hydra as a female. What do you think about this? How is Hydra like a female? Does gender matter for mythical creatures? (Gender means male or female.)

Learn More

- Evslin, Bernard. *The Hydra*. New York: Chelsea House Publications, 1989.
- Kelly, Sophia. *What a Beast! A Look-It-Up Guide to the Monsters and Mutants of Mythology*. New York: Scholastic Library Publishing, 2010.
- Knudsen, Shannon. *Fantastical Creatures and Magical Beasts*. Minneapolis: Lerner Publications, 2009.
- McKerley, Jennifer Guess. *Hydra*. San Diego: KidHaven, 2009.

Glossary

acid (AS-id) poison that can burn through things

centaur (SEN-tor) human with a horse body

dragon (DRAG-uhn) mythical monster that looks like a giant reptile

immortal (ih-MOR-tuhl) ability to live forever

regenerate (rih-JEN-uh-rate) to regrow body parts

siblings (SIB-lingz) brothers and sisters

slayed (SLAYD) killed

underworld (UHN-der-wurld) mythological place where people went after they died

Index

About the Author

Dr. Virginia Loh-Hagan is an author, university professor, former classroom teacher, and curriculum designer. Before writing this book, she didn't know what hydras were. She lives in San Diego with her very tall husband and very naughty dogs. To learn more about her, visit www.virginialoh.com.